THAT'S ME IN HISTORY

THE SPANISH EMPIRE

THE INQUISITION

Tamra Orr

PURPLE TOAD
PUBLISHING

P.O. Box 631
Kennett Square, Pennsylvania 19348
www.purpletoadpublishing.com

Ancient Egypt
Medieval England
Ming Dynasty China
Renaissance Italy
The Spanish Empire: The Inquisition

ABOUT THE AUTHOR: Tamra Orr is a full-time author living in the Pacific Northwest with her husband, children, cat, and dog. She graduated from Ball State University in Muncie, Indiana. She has written more than 300 books about many subjects, ranging from historical events and career choices to controversial issues and biographies. On those rare occasions that she is not writing a book, she is reading one.

Printing   1   2   3   4   5   6   7   8   9

Orr, Tamra
  The Spanish Empire: The Inquisition / Tamra Orr
    p. cm. — (That's me in history)
Includes bibliographic references and index.
ISBN: 978-1-62469-048-8 (library bound)
1. Inquisition—Spain—Juvenile literature.   I. Title.
  BX1735 2013
  272.20946—dc23
                                                    2013936505

eBook ISBN: 9781624690495

Printed by Lake Book Manufacturing, Chicago, IL

CONTENTS

Get Out!

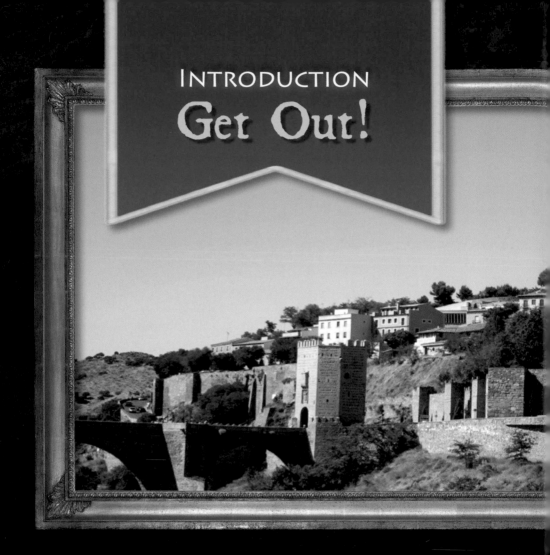

I felt the warm sunshine of the early spring morning soaking into my skin. Beautiful mornings were nothing unusual in Spain, but this one seemed almost perfect. I began shaking out the rug I had pulled outside. I smiled at the clouds of dust it sent scurrying up into the air. Some glittered in the sunlight like jewels.

What was that? It sounded like hurried footsteps coming my way. I glanced up to see Papa and David striding toward the house. Papa was never home at this time of day. He was usually in the city, buying seeds and talking of farming. My brother David should have been with Rabbi Ira in school. Why were they both home?

According to some, Jews had lived throughout Spanish towns for 15 centuries. They lived peacefully among the city's Muslim and Christian populations.

"Papa . . ." My voice trailed off as I caught sight of his face. He looked terribly frightened. I had never, ever seen Papa scared, not even when David had been so sick we thought we would lose him. Papa was the strongest man I knew, able to work harder and longer than anyone. Yet his eyes were wide and full of tears. David was pale and would not meet my eyes. My stomach turned with worry.

Papa rushed into the house in search of Mama. I followed, knowing it was best to stay quiet.

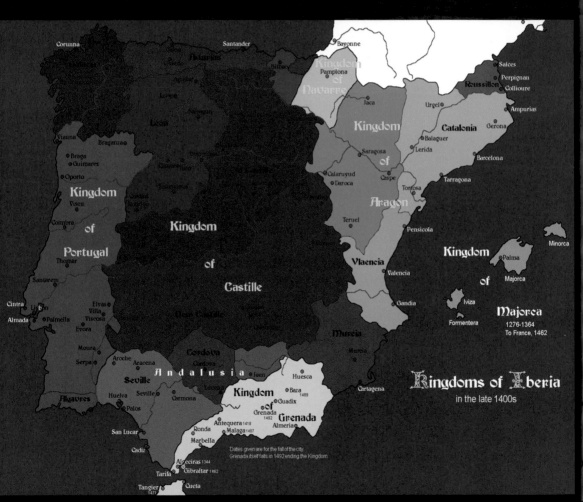

Kingdoms of Iberia
in the late 1400s

Dates given are for the fall of the city.
Grenada itself falls in 1492 ending the Kingdom

In the late 1400s, Spain was divided into six kingdoms, with the Kingdom of Castille covering the greatest amount of territory.

"Eli, why are you . . . ?" Mama asked, and then she saw the look on his face. "Eli, what is wrong? What has happened? Why is David not in school?"

Papa sat down at the table and reached for Mama's hand. Grasping tightly, he said, "The king has finally done it, Leah. He has ordered us all out." His voice caught. "We have three months to prepare."

Mama put her head down and sobbed. Seeing her cry was as rare as seeing Papa frightened. I could not stay silent any longer.

"What are you talking about, Papa?" I asked. "David, what did the king say? Why must we go?"

"The king has issued a formal edict, Rifka. All Jews have been ordered out of Spain," David said quietly.

"What did the order say, Eli?" asked Mama.

"It was so final and cold," replied Papa. "It was addressed to 'all Jews and Jewesses of whatever age they may be,' and said we must depart or else"—he paused a moment—"or else we will 'incur the penalty of death and the confiscation' of all we own." [1] I felt as if I could not breathe. Leave my home? My belongings? My friends? Why? I could not imagine any of it. I loved my country. It was full of such beauty and wonder and I was happy here. Why would King Ferdinand and Queen Isabella tell us we have to leave? I had never even seen the king or queen. Where, oh where, would we go?

I reached out and grabbed David's hand. Usually he did not like that, but today, the 31st of March, 1492, was different. This time he held on just as tightly. Our lives were about to change and there was nothing we could do about it.

CHAPTER 1

Of Columbus and Conversos

Hello! My name is Rifka, and I am ten years old. That awful day in March was one I will remember for the rest of my life. As you probably noticed, I did not understand exactly what was going on, but since then, I have learned all about the king's edict and what it means for my family. It means we have to leave the only land I have ever known.

Every moment since the Alhambra Decree, as everyone is calling it, has been uncertain. In town, Papa says everyone is talking about an explorer named Christopher Columbus. The king and queen have given Columbus permission to sail three of their ships, the *Niña*, the *Pinta*, and the *Santa Maria*, in search of a new route to China. Everyone seems to be wondering what he will find.

In our village, Columbus is ignored and everyone is arguing about what to do about

Christopher Columbus begged the king and queen for the chance to travel the seas in search of a new trade route to Asia. His voyage would change the history of the world.

The young Isabella and Ferdinand of Castile made a number of decisions that rippled through Spain. They expanded their empire, helped unite kingdoms, and forced non-Christians out of the country.

the decree. Papa said some of our greatest teachers and leaders went to the palace to beg the king to change his mind, but it did not work. These men even gathered great sums of money and offered it to the throne, but were refused.[1]

Seal of the Tribunal for the Holy Office of the Inquisition

My next door neighbor is Beth Rahamin. We have been friends since I can remember. When I asked her if she was packing like we were, I was shocked to hear her family was not leaving Spain.

"Papa says we have too much here to walk away from," said Beth. "Who will harvest the field we have worked so hard to farm? How can we move all of our things? Plus Grandmother Tevya could never survive the trip. We will convert."

I did not know what to say. I knew that some of the Jews had decided to convert to Christianity so they could stay in Spain, but Papa had told David and me that doing so betrayed our God, our faith, and our people. I tried to imagine never again lighting the menorah candles for Hanukkah or working during Shabbat instead of resting. Passover would never mean the same thing if Papa did not stand up at the Seder and tell of our people's exodus from Egypt so long ago. I knew nothing about how to celebrate the Christians' Christmas, Easter, or Lent. I knew in town, during the last week of Lent, women wore lacy mantillas on their heads

Many families at the time honored Passover and held it close to their hearts as they celebrated it in secret.

and people paraded through the streets.[2] I preferred my quiet time at home with the simple light of candles and storytelling.

"You are going to become a . . . Converso?" I asked, horrified. We had all heard the rumors of these Crypto-Jews. They swore they were Christians and attended the Catholic Church, but the throne still did not trust them. The king and queen suspected the converts were only pretending to follow Christianity while they secretly kept following the rules of the Jewish faith. I had even heard that people from the church would force their way into people's homes to make sure they were making pork for dinner. Our people are not allowed to eat it, so having pork for a meal proved the Conversos were turning their backs on their old ways.

Medieval Spanish altarpieces like this one show how Christians wanted Jews to convert. At first it was a request, but later Jews had no choice in the matter. They were evicted from the country and their synagogues, or churches, were taken over by Christian leaders.

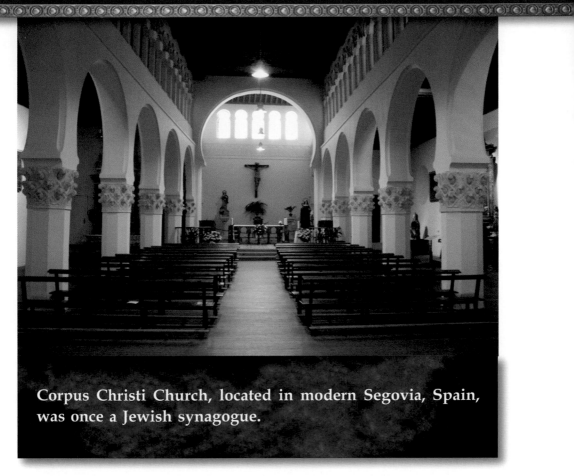

Corpus Christi Church, located in modern Segovia, Spain, was once a Jewish synagogue.

"The Church does not trust Conversos," I added. "Did you not hear just last week Ezra Yamin was taken by force for questioning? When people are taken by the Church, they do not return." I begged Beth to join us, but she refused, even though she seemed unsure.

I hugged her and wondered if I would ever see her again. I doubted it. In a matter of weeks, we would leave, and I did not even know our destination. I could only hope we would find a new home and that Beth's family would be able to keep theirs.

THE GOLDEN AGE OF SPANISH JEWRY

In the year 711, Moors, Muslims from North Africa, rode into Spain and claimed it for themselves. They controlled the land for almost 800 years and called it Al-Andalus.[3] The Muslims believed strongly in religious tolerance. While they followed a religion known as Islam, they were also willing to accept those who made other choices. Muslims, Christians, and Jews all got along although they lived in separate areas. Not only were they allowed to practice their religions in peace, the Jews also became rich, successfu, and happy. Life was so good that the tenth, eleventh, and twelfth centuries are often referred to as the Golden Age of Jewry.

During this Golden Age, Jews changed the world in many ways. They worked as diplomats and ambassadors to Muslim caliphs, or leaders. Some owned thriving businesses. Others became merchants, traveling the world to buy and trade silk, spices, timber, and other treasures.

Many Jews made important changes in the fields of astronomy, medicine, and philosophy. They invented instruments used by sailors to navigate the oceans, including the astrolabe and quadrant. Both tools were used to measure the angles of the sun and stars so that ship captains knew which ways to sail when crossing the open seas.[4]

In 1147, another group of Muslims rode into Spain. Known as Almohads, they were the opposite of the Moors. Rather than have religious tolerance, they insisted their religion was the only right one. Jews were insulted, ridiculed, and treated terribly. To make matters worse, a number of disasters struck Spain. In the early fourteenth

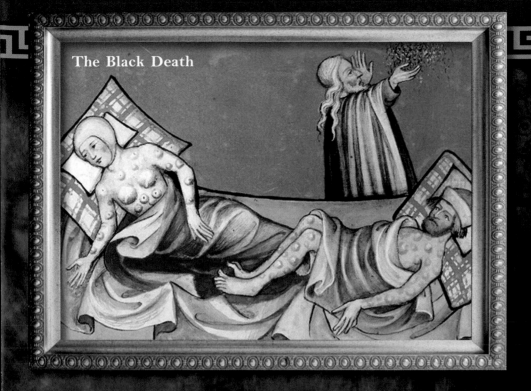

The Black Death

century, the coldest, harshest winter in history created widespread famine. The extra snow then turned into spring flooding.

Then the worst catastrophe of all hit—the Black Plague. An infection carried by fleas traveling on rats, the plague spread to humans and swept through Asia and Europe. Experts estimate that more than 25 million people died.[5] The year 1348 was especially brutal, with more people dying in four months than in the previous 20 years.

Famine, floods—and then, finally, pestilence. People were suffering and dying. They needed someone or something to blame, and they chose the Jewish people. False rumors began to circulate about Jewish doctors who put poison under their fingernails to kill Christian patients. Other people whispered that Jews were planning to poison the water supply.[6] Suddenly, the Jews were seen as villains. Their lives began to change quickly from this point and not for the better. The Golden Age was over.

CHAPTER 2

The Beauty of Spain

It is getting harder to remember what life was like before the edict. Sometimes I dream about those days. I never thought I would miss doing my usual chores, but I do.

Come into our home. It is simple, like most of those around us. I remember watching Papa and David build it. They used mud and pebbles that dried into bricks. Every few years, they would repair them. Days of hot sun or hard rain would make our home fall apart. I had hoped to help the next time we had to fix it, but I knew now that that chance would never come.

Have you seen some of the fancier homes in the city? They are much bigger, with two stories, and many are made of stone. When Papa and I would walk by, I would peek through the open doors to see walls covered in tapestries and floors

The beauty of Medieval Spain can still be seen in twelfth-century bridges like this one in Girona, Catalonia, Spain.

Elegant tapestries made of wool and silk like this one from the 15th century tell the history of Spain in rich color and detail.

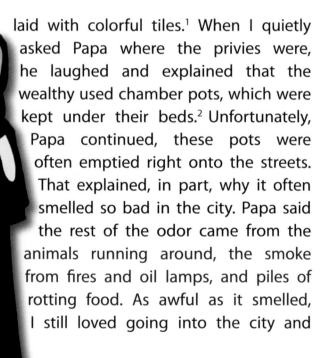

laid with colorful tiles.[1] When I quietly asked Papa where the privies were, he laughed and explained that the wealthy used chamber pots, which were kept under their beds.[2] Unfortunately, Papa continued, these pots were often emptied right onto the streets. That explained, in part, why it often smelled so bad in the city. Papa said the rest of the odor came from the animals running around, the smoke from fires and oil lamps, and piles of rotting food. As awful as it smelled, I still loved going into the city and

In many places in Spain, laws forced Jews to wear yellow circles on their clothing to clearly identify them from the rest of the people.

seeing how other people lived. It was like an adventure every time.

One time in town, Papa stopped to talk to someone, and I was drawn by the towering cathedral under construction. It was almost finished. It was immense, with angels carved of stone over the arched doorways, and frightening gargoyles on the corners. I peeked inside to see if there were any of the religious paintings or tapestries I had heard covered the walls. Before my eyes could

Many of Spain's cathedrals were covered in fancy carvings on the outside and in rich tapestries on the inside.

adjust to the darkness inside, I felt Papa's hand on my arm. "This is not a place for us, Rifka," he said sternly, pulling me away.

On another trip, I had gotten a glimpse of one of the king's many castles. The courtyard had been buzzing like a beehive with people selling food and drink, and officers waiting to see the king. Nobles walked through, adorned in bright damask shirts with fur trim.[3] I even saw some knights wearing their shiny armor. They rattled as they walked by. It was amazing. I almost stopped breathing when one of the bishops passed in front of me. I wanted to reach out and touch the silk and velvet of his robes. How different they looked from our rabbis, who dressed in long black gowns.

The King and Queen's Alcazar Castle in Segovia is one of the most ornate and artistic buildings in all of Spain.

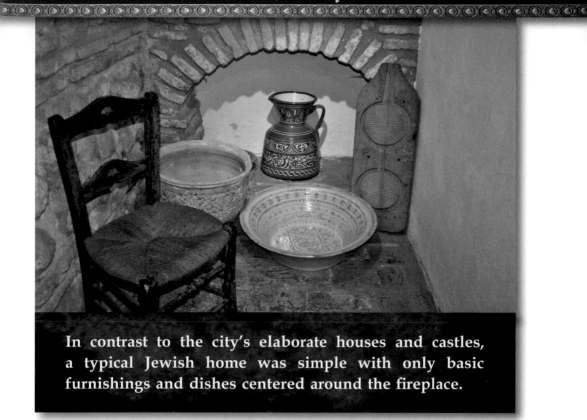

In contrast to the city's elaborate houses and castles, a typical Jewish home was simple with only basic furnishings and dishes centered around the fireplace.

Despite what I saw in the city, I was always happy to return home. Our house has a large room in the middle where we sit to eat. On one wall is the fireplace, where fires keep us warm in the winter and where we cook most of our meals. The other rooms are where we sleep. We have mattresses on the floor. Our privy is out back, and I try never to have to use it after dark. I am very grateful it is David's chore to clean it and spread the waste on the fields as fertilizer.

Papa grew wheat in the field behind our home. He also had cattle, sheep, and chickens he watched over. Even though he frowned at me, I often gave the animals names. Half of everything we earned from the wheat and animals went to our landlord.[4] It paid for us to live in our little house. The rest of our money I knew went for seeds and equipment. Now, as the time to leave

One of the richest meals made in Jewish homes was cholent. This stew was made with beef or chicken, potatoes, beans and rice or barley. Often whole eggs, still in their shells, were added to the stew and cooked. By morning, they would be brown and ready to eat.

approaches, I am saying goodbye to all of our animals. They will remain with the house. I will miss them—along with many things I will miss about my home. Only the mule we were given will make the journey with us.

Mama taught me how to take care of the house. I know how to cook meat although we rarely eat it. Lamb is my favorite. I do not like goat—it's too stringy. Mama makes cholent often, a stew made from a combination of cabbage, onions, beans, peas, and breadcrumbs. Before Shabbat, she makes a fresh batch that will simmer throughout the holy day of rest.

For the last two years, I have baked all of our bread. It has filled the house with the most wonderful scents. Do you like

Traditional honeycake

biscuits and scones? I love them. Usually I make loaves of dark rye, but sometimes I make cakes sweetened with honey to sell at the market.

"Rifka, Papa and I are going out to check the traps for rabbits," David said yesterday as he walked by. I knew he was trying to be brave, but he was also sad. He misses his friends. He is used to going to school every day to learn about the Torah and Talmud from Rabbi Ira. He always came home to help Papa, and the two would talk nonstop about religious questions and laws. David had just started learning Hebrew. He loves speaking it with Papa and checking to see if he is saying it correctly. Spending the day plowing, planting, herding animals, sheering sheep, and checking traps is not nearly as exciting for him.

"Help me chop vegetables for the stew, Rifka," Mama calls from inside the house. "Then, we must go back to separating what we are going to sell, and what we will take with us on our journey." She sighs. I know this is a difficult time for her as well. We do not own much, but what we have is precious. It is hard to decide what to take and what to leave behind.

THE MARRIAGE OF FERDINAND AND ISABELLA

The marriage of Ferdinand and Isabella changed the history of Spain. The two leaders are usually remembered for their support of Christopher Columbus's exploratory voyage to America. With their efforts and his claim on the New World, the Spanish Empire eventually spread across five continents and lasted 500 years.

Isabella and Ferdinand met on October 16, 1469, and three days later they were married. Isabella was a mere eighteen years old. Ferdinand was only seventeen! Because they were first cousins, the two had to get church permission and married in secret.[5]

When the king and queen came into power, Spain was still under the rule of the Muslims, and had been for almost 800 years. As devout Catholics, Isabella and Ferdinand felt the only way to make Spain a strong country was to ensure the people all shared the same faith. The first order of business was fighting the Muslims. For ten years, the Spanish throne, urged by the powerful Catholic Church, battled the last stronghold of Muslims in the kingdom of Granada. In January 1492, Granada finally fell.[6]

At first, the Jews had not feared the new rulers. Isabella had even sworn to protect the Jewish people. Over time, however, the Catholic Church gained more and more power. Knowing that the monarchs wanted a unified country, the Church convinced them to go after the Jews next. If they did not, the Church assured the throne that the Jews would be a constant threat. Their differences would pick and pull at the threads of Spain's control, and slowly unravel it. If everyone had the same religion, the Church said, there would be less conflict. The kingdom would be peaceful and far easier to control. At last, Ferdinand and Isabella agreed.

After issuing the Alhambra Decree, the Jewish people had three choices. They could choose to convert to Christianity, they would be forced to convert, or they had to leave.

The two teenagers married in secret and then changed all of Spain with their passion for uniting the kingdoms under one faith.

About half of the 80,000 Jews willingly converted.[7] These Conversos, or Crypto-Jews, were always under suspicion. Had they chosen to be Christians because of a true change in faith—or because they did not want to leave Spain? The Jews who were forced to convert through torture were distrusted even more. Had they honestly had a change of heart, or were they desperate to put an end to their rulers' painful torture methods?

The other half of the Jews decided to leave Spain. They sold their homes for whatever they were able to get, which was often little more than a mule to help them carry their belongings.[8] They were not allowed to take gold, silver, or jewels out of Spain. They had to either sell them or give them to those staying behind. When a rumor went around that some Jews were swallowing gold pieces and jewelry in order to smuggle them out of the country, thieves began hiding along the road waiting for them. As Jews walked past, these criminals would leap out and cut the people open, hoping to find treasure still inside them.[9]

CHAPTER 3

Suspicion Everywhere

I woke yesterday to the sound of yelling outside. I jumped up from my mattress and grabbed my wool tunic and skirt. David and I almost bumped into each other running to the front door.

"Who was that?" I asked quietly.

"I think it was Solomon Rahamin," he whispered back.

Beth's father? I closed my eyes and prayed for her family's safety.

"Do not open the door, Rifka," said Mama. "Stay quiet."

We listened carefully. The Inquisitor General's men, called familiars, were questioning Beth's family. They sounded cruel and I knew Beth must be terrified. Tears ran down my face as I listened carefully to Beth's father answering the inquisitors' questions as simply as he could.

The hooded and cloaked familiars of the Inquisition struck terror in everyone's hearts. They were often cruel and happy to resort to physical torture in order to get the answers they were searching for.

Torture would soon follow for those found to be practicing Judaism.

Suddenly we heard the question we had all feared. "What of your neighbors? Are they heretics as well, Rahamin? Do they light candles on Friday? Does the wife clean the house that day? Do they follow the ways of Judaism?"

Can you imagine how frightened we felt at that moment? I could hear Mama holding her breath behind me. The answer to that question could change our lives in a second. Instead of packing for our journey, we would find ourselves being hauled away for questioning.

"No, no . . . the Meyers are Conversos, like us," replied Rahamin. "We converted at the same time."

Mama, David, and I let out a breath of relief together. For now, we were safe. The Rahamins were not, though. Solomon was taken away for further questioning. I hoped he would return safely.

"We must hurry," said Mama. "We leave by sunrise."

The rest of the day, we worked to get ready to leave. We had a mule to carry some of our belongings. The house, as well as the cattle, sheep, and chickens, would return to the landlord. I had given some of my possessions away to Beth.

Before the sun rose this morning, Mama shook my shoulder to wake me. "It is time," she said. In the predawn darkness, Papa,

Mama, David, and I said goodbye to our house. Softly, we crept next door and Papa knocked lightly on the Rahamins' door.

"Esther," Papa said, "we can never thank you enough for what Solomon did for us when the inquisitors were here." He paused. "We cannot take our jewels with us, so Leah and I want to give you what little we have." He handed her several gold pieces, and the ring I knew was once Grandma Reyna's.

"Oh Eli . . . ," she said, at a loss for words. Mama reached over and hugged her tightly. I knew that said more than any words possibly could.

Now, as the sun rises, I feel my spirits rising with it. We have joined with others walking forward, leaving Spain behind. I am sad to leave my beautiful country, but grateful that my family is together. Walk with us as we go in search of a new life.

The journey from Spain was a painful one for families. They were often torn between the grief of leaving their homes and the gratitude of keeping their families together.

THE TECHNIQUES OF TORTURE

The Spanish Inquisition began in 1481 under the direction of a cruel and determined priest named Tómas de Torquemada. His actions were approved by the Catholic Church and by the king and queen. The Inquisition was enacted to make sure that the Conversos were sincere and were not secretly practicing Jewish traditions at home.[1]

Torquemada, the Inquisitor General, believed it would take far more than mere questions to get to the truth. His methods were cruel. During his 18 years in power, 2,000 people were burned alive. More than 17,000 were injured. The general's name was enough to strike terror in the hearts of anyone who heard it.

To help him track down any suspicious people, Torquemada used officers called familiars. Dressed in black cloaks, these men went into homes, churches, and anywhere else they wanted. Former nobles, they were given extra privileges and honors.

Being grabbed by a familiar was terrifying. Unlike today, the accused In Spain had no rights. They did not know why they were being questioned or what crime they supposedly committed. Though pressured to confess, most of the time, the accused did not know what to confess to.

Once taken to a cell, people were chained, left alone, and not allowed to speak or have any visitors. Questioning was done in a darkened room. Windows were covered with black curtains. Candles flickered, casting shadows in the corners. Hour after hour, men in white robes with black hoods over their faces asked confusing questions. These methods were designed to confuse people into confessing a sin or into turning over their friends, family, and neighbors.[2]

The experience did not end with simple questioning. Torture followed. Some had their hands and feet tied to a wooden rack and were stretched

A variety of torture techniques were used in order to extract the information the kingdom required. Many people confessed to anything they could in order to stop the pain.

until their joints separated. Others endured a water torture called *taca*. Strapped down, the person's head was held, nostrils plugged, and jaws forced open. A piece of fabric was laid over the mouth, and then water was poured slowly into the cloth. The water pushed it lower and lower into the throat until the person could no longer breathe.[3]

Believe it or not, the goal of torture was not to kill prisoners, but to get confessions. If a person confessed but did not convert, they were punished at a public gathering known as the *auto de fe,* or act of faith.[4] The guilty were paraded into the city. Their crimes and their punishments were read aloud. These gatherings served as warnings to others. The convicts were led away to face their sentences out of sight. Some were whipped, but many were also burned alive.[5] Their ashes were spread in the fields so there would be no trace of them left.[6] By the end of the Inquisition in the early 1800s, experts believe, nearly 32,000 people had been tortured to death.[7]

CHAPTER 4

Journey into the Unknown

"Rifka, walk faster!" David keeps saying. "We are almost there and you are falling behind."

I want to hurry, but my feet feel like they weigh at least fifty pounds. It feels as if we have been walking forever. I am still excited for what lies ahead, but I want to be there already so I can sit down and enjoy it.

"Children, we are there at last," says Papa, pointing ahead. We have finally reached one of the harbors on the Mediterranean Sea. We are obviously not the only ones who want to sail to a new land. The harbor is bursting with people, all of them looking as tired as we are.

"Look at the ships, Mama!" I say. Every inch of the coastline is lined with ships in all shapes and sizes. The captains call out from each one, offering trips across the sea.

"They look like vultures," Papa mutters to Mama.

Many different kinds of ships crossed the ocean during the 14th and 15th centuries, including the six-sailed carrack and the caravel, a trade ship used by Columbus and other explorers.

"I know," she answers, "and I am not sure if this makes me feel better or worse."

Mama and I find a place to sit down and rest while Papa and David go to speak with the ship captains. Almost an hour passes before they return.

"We have found passage at last." Papa sighs as he slumps to the ground. "We no longer have a mule or much money, but we have a way across the sea. We leave in two hours."

Mama and Papa lie down to nap, but I keep looking around. This is one of the most exciting places I have ever seen. One boat unloads the day's catch onto the docks. The silver scales of the

This is a replica of Columbus's ship, the Santa Maria. It was a style of ship known as the carrack, a three- or four-masted sailing ship first designed by the Portuguese.

Harbor towns, like the port of Palo de la Frontera where Columbus departed from, were often bustling and loud as people landed in Spain or left for other adventures and explorations.

fish flash in the sunshine. When Mama and I had prepared dishes with flounder or sole, I never imagined the fish coming to shore in such huge nets. A few feet away, two men are arguing over the price of the spices that have just arrived from India. It reminds me of Columbus and his search for a quicker route to the East in order to speed up the spice trade. I heard that some of the sailors are paid in cloves![1] The business of the harbors reminds me of the palace courtyard. It is noisy, confusing, colorful, and endlessly fascinating.

Hurry! It is finally time to board. More and more people are lining up behind us. Will we run out of room? Will the boat sink with so many people?

WELCOMING THE SEPHARDIM

Where do thousands of Jews go when they are told to leave their country? These people wondered the same thing. About 10,000 of these *Sephardim,* as this group of Jews came to be called, headed to Italy.[2] Many of the Italian cities refused to let them in. Places that did welcome them, including Naples and Venice, later turned them out just as other European nations had done. (England had cast them out in 1290, and France in 1302.)

From Spain, a large group went to Portugal. Although they were allowed in, they had to pay a fee and could stay only eight months at the longest. Five years later, Portugal's leader, Manuel I, was offered Ferdinand and Isabella's daughter's hand in marriage. She was his on one condition: Manuel had to expel all of the Jews living in Portugal. He agreed, but the Jews refused to leave. Finally, Manuel gathered as many Jewish children as he could find, and had them baptized by force. Later their parents were baptized also, turning all of them into Conversos.[3]

Other Jews decided to cross the Mediterranean Sea and go to North Africa. Sea captains took advantage of the travelers' panic. They crowded the harbors with ships, each one promising a fast, safe voyage. Sadly, a number of these sailors were lying. Some were pushed overboard.[4] Others were killed by pirates. Those who actually made it to the shores of North Africa were still not out of danger. Robbers and murderers waited for them on the beaches. Food and water were

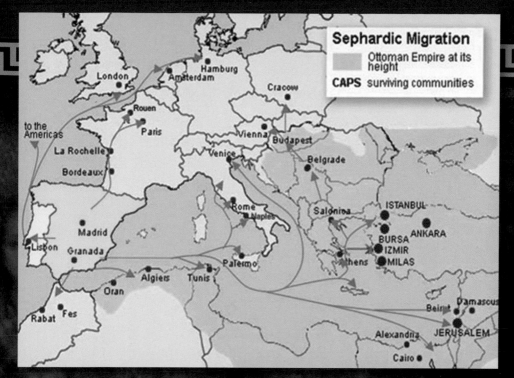

Sephardic Migration

Ottoman Empire at its height

CAPS surviving communities

The migration of the Jews sent them in many directions and to different lands, affecting each country's culture from its traditions to its cuisine.

scarce, and it was not unknown for starving Jews to become a meal for the area's lions and bears.[5]

One of the safest places for Jews at this time was the Ottoman Empire, including southwest Asia and northeast Africa. A number of Jews already lived in these areas, and they helped those who were running from Spain. Sultan Bayezid II opened his gates to all Jewish travelers, saying, "It is strictly forbidden for the rulers of any Ottoman community to refuse entry to any Jews, but they should be received with open arms and friendliness. Anyone who disobeys this order will be subject to the death penalty."[6]

Jews changed the history of this part of the world. By the early 1500s, many of them had settled in Istanbul. That community became the largest Jewish group in the world.[7]

CHAPTER 5

Land, Ho!

Good morning! When I first opened my eyes at dawn, I did not remember where I was. Home? On the road? Ah no, we are still on the ship. It has been a long journey.

I was right to worry although I worried about the wrong things. There were too many people on the ship, but it did not sink. Instead, people who gave the captain trouble were thrown overboard. Papa told us every morning to stay quiet and ask for nothing. "We are not troublemakers," he said. "Pray that the journey goes fast and we reach shore without any problems."

One morning we were awakened by the cry of "Fire!" An onboard fire was a captain's biggest fear. David ran to help carry buckets of ocean water to put it out. We heard the sailors telling stories of ships that had not been as fortunate. We also

The North African coast
promised newfound safety that
many Jewish families prayed for.

heard tales of ships that ran out of food and water, and others that sank before reaching shore. Passengers whispered of cities that demanded high payment in order to be allowed in. Other cities were so frightened that passengers might be carrying the Black Death that they let no one come shore. I closed my eyes and prayed none of this happened to us.

Now I am smiling as I remember the dream I had about guitar music. I had heard the song when I was last in the city with Papa. It was wild and fast and had made me want to dance. Although it was fun, I preferred the music of my people. It was created with rare and precious instruments like violins, clarinets, and accordions.[1] I had heard it played at a wedding and now those notes floated in and out of my memory.

A Sephardic woman sang and tapped her tambourine to the beat. She had performed

Fretless lute used in Sephardic music

in many weddings throughout her life. Women like her are known as *tanyderas* and they play an important role in Sephardic weddings. I hoped to myself that one day a tanydera might sing at my own wedding.

At last we hear the call we have been waiting for: "Land, ho!" See the coastline way in the distance? I am so eager to put my feet on the ground again. I have had enough of the sea for now. What will life be like in Northern Africa? Can you imagine? I am more than ready to find out.

"Rifka, take this," Mama says. She hands me one of the rugs we have brought with us. I smile and begin shaking out the rug, watching dust clouds dance in the morning sunshine.

Thank you for going on this incredible journey with me. It is clear that life is changing by the moment for us right now, but some things have stayed just the same.

What new life awaits on the near coastline?

FALL OF THE SPANISH EMPIRE

For much of Spain, Christopher Columbus's voyage was important news. Although he was searching for a quicker route to China, he found the continent of North America. Until then, the only land Spain owned outside of Europe was the Canary Islands. Columbus's voyage changed all that. By the middle of the sixteenth century, Spain had grown immensely in power. It controlled large areas of South America, Italy, Austria, and the Netherlands, as well as most of Mexico and Central America.

Spain's rulers, one after the next, believed God had chosen them to control larger and larger parts of the world. They sent explorers to find land and claim it. They sent conquistadors to win land from the native people. These ruthless men did not hesitate to kill the people they met. Torture was common, but the smallpox disease that these Spanish soldiers brought did the most damage to cultures like the Aztecs and the Incas.[2] The Spanish throne also sent Catholic missionaries to convert people to Christianity. Spanish missions were built in many parts of America. The idea to unify the empire through shared religion was still strong. Weak leaders, damaging wars, and passionate rebellions against the crown finally brought the Spanish Empire to an end in

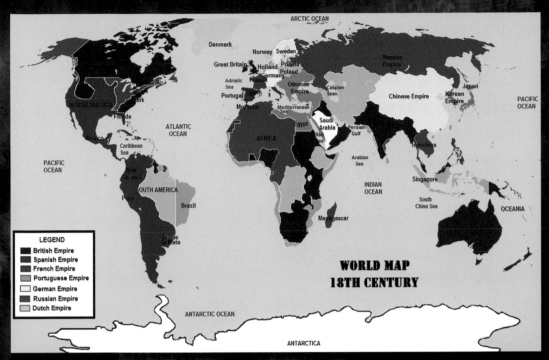

By the start of the 18th century, Spain controlled large portions of land in North, Central, and South America.

1898, but its influence is still felt today. Spain is part of the European Union. Its former colonies, now independent, are still flavored by the foods and traditions of Spain. In 2013, the first Spanish Pope in over 500 years was chosen to lead the worldwide Catholic population. Pope Francis is from Argentina—the first Pope from Latin America.

711   Muslims take over Spain and rule for almost 800 years.

1147   The Almohad Muslims take over part of Spain.

1290   England expels all Jews.

1306   France expels all Jews.

1348   The Black Death reaches Spain.

1469   Ferdinand and Isabella are married.

1474   The reign of Ferdinand and Isabella begins.

1481   The Spanish Inquisition begins, and the first auto de fe is held.

1492   Columbus sets sail, discovering America; the Alhambra Decree is enacted, forcing the Jews from Spain; the last Muslim kingdom falls, and the Spanish Empire begins to grow.

1497   Portugal expels all Jews.

1513   Vasco Nuñez de Balboa reaches the Pacific Coast of the Americas and claims it for Spain.

1515   Spain conquers Cuba and establishes the town of Havana.

1521   Hernan Cortes establishes Spanish control over Mexico.

1537   Spain has full control of Peru.

1571   Spain takes control of the Philippines.

1774   Spain occupies the Falkland Islands.

1812   Spain recovers control of Venezuela.

1826   The last auto de fe is held.

1834   The Inquisition is abolished.

1836   At the Battle of the Alamo, Texas fails to gain independence from Mexico.

1884   Spain colonizes the Western Sahara.

1898   Spain loses the Spanish-American War and yields its colonies north of the Rio Grande to the United States; the Spanish Empire comes to an end.

Introduction: Get Out!
1. Dennis Cummings, "On This Day: Jews Banished from Spain during Spanish Inquisition," *Finding Dulcinea*, March 31, 2011.

Chapter 1. Of Columbus and Conversos
1. James M. Anderson, *Daily Life in the Spanish Inquisition* (Westport, CT: Greenwood Press, 2002), p. 98.
2. "Foreign News: Mantilla Week." *Time*, April 28, 1930.
3. Norman Berdichevsky, "The Myth of the Golden Age of Tolerance in Medieval Muslim Spain," *New English Review*, November 2006.
4. Samuel Kurinsky, "Jews and Navigation," Hebrew History Federation.
5. "Plague: The Black Death," *National Geographic*.
6. Nancy Rubin, *Isabella of Castile: The First Renaissance Queen* (Lincoln, Nebraska: iUniverse, 2004), p. 298.

Chapter 2. The Beauty of Spain
1. James M. Anderson, *Daily Life in the Spanish Inquisition* (Westport, CT: Greenwood Press, 2002), p. 134.
2. Ibid., p. 135.
3. Jarob Sacudeo, "Types of Clothing of the Middle Ages," *Bright Hub Education*, December 27, 2011.
4. Anderson, p. 157.
5. PBS, "When Worlds Collide: The Untold Story of the Americas after Columbus," PBS.org, undated.
6. Ibid.
7. Anderson, p. 99.
8. Ibid.
9. Ulick Ralph Burke, *A History of Spain from the Earliest Times to the Death of Ferdinand the Catholic* (London: Longmans, Green and Co., 1900), p. 127.

Chapter 3. Suspicion Everywhere
1. James M. Anderson, *Daily Life in the Spanish Inquisition* (Westport, CT: Greenwood Press, 2002), pp. 62–66.
2. Ibid., p. 67.
3. Ibid., pp. 67–68.
4. Ibid., pp. 69–70.
5. "The Inquisition," *Jewish Virtual Library*, undated.
6. "Introduction to Inquisition Auto de Fe Records," Rare Books and Special Collections, Hesburgh Libraries of Notre Dame.
7. "Spain, the Jews, the Spanish Inquisition, and After."

Chapter 4. Journey into the Unknown
1. The Silk Road Spice Merchants, "History of the Spice Trade," *The Silk Road*.
2. James M. Anderson, *Daily Life in the Spanish Inquisition* (Westport, CT: Greenwood Press, 2002), p. 99.
3. "Portugal," Early Modern Jewish History.
4. "Tisha B'Av," The Jewish Community Center of Harrison, August 2, 2012.
5. Anderson, p. 100.
6. Rabbi Chaim Schloss, *2000 Years of Jewish History* (Jerusalem, Israel: Feldheim Publishers: 2002), pp. 139–140.
7. "Ottoman Empire," Early Modern Jewish History.

Chapter 5. Land, Ho!
1. "Hebrew Music and Jewish Music." Music Stack.
2. Marc Eliany, "A Brief Social History of the Jews in Morocco."

Books

Engel, Barbara, et al. *From Ur to Eternity, Vol. 1: From Patriarchs to the Spanish Inquisition.* Jersey City, NJ: KTAV Publishing House, 2010.

Stein, Conrad. *The Conquistadores: Building a Spanish Empire in the Americas.* North Mankato, MN: The Child's World, 2004.

Worth, Richard. *The Spanish Inquisition in World History.* Berkeley Heights, NJ: Enslow Publishers, 2002.

Zinn, Howard. *A Young People's History of the United States: Columbus to the War on Terror.* New York: Seven Stories Press, 2009.

Works Consulted

Anderson, James M. *Daily Life During the Spanish Inquisition.* Westport, CT: Greenwood Press, 2002.

Berdichevsky, Norman. "The Myth of the Golden Age of Tolerance in Medieval Muslim Spain." *New English Review,* November 2006. http://www.newenglishreview.org/Norman_Berdichevsky/The_Myth_of_the_Golden_Age_of_Tolerance_in_Medieval_Muslim_Spain/

Burke, Ulick Ralph. *A History of Spain from the Earliest Times to the Death of Ferdinand the Catholic.* London: Longmans, Green and Co., 1900.

Cummings, Dennis. "On This Day: Jews Banished from Spain during Spanish Inquisition." *Finding Dulcinea,* March 31, 2011. http://www.findingdulcinea.com/news/on-this-day/March/Jews-Banished-From-Spain-During-Spanish-Inquisition.html

Early Modern Jewish History. Wesleyan University, 2009. http://jewishhistory.research.wesleyan.edu/

Eliany, Marc. "A Brief Social History of the Jews in Morocco." http://artengine.ca/eliany/html/mindandsoulinjewishmorocco/historyofjewsinmorocco.html

"Foreign News: Mantilla Week." *Time,* April 28, 1930. http://www.time.com/time/magazine/article/0,9171,752437,00.html

Forward.com. "Recalling the Golden Days of Spain." *The Jewish Daily Forward,* January 3, 2003. http://forward.com/articles/9066/recalling-the-golden-days-of-spain/

Gitlitz, David. *A Drizzle of Honey: The Lives and Recipes of Spain's Secret Jews.* New York: St. Martin's Press, 1999.

"Hebrew Music and Jewish Music." *Music Stack.* http://www.musicstack.com/genre/hewbrew

"The Inquisition." Jewish Virtual Library, undated. http://www.jewishvirtuallibrary.org/jsource/History/Inquisition.html

"Introduction to Inquisition Auto de Fe Records." Rare Books and Special Collections, Hesburgh Libraries of Notre Dame. http://www.library.nd.edu/rarebooks/digital_projects/inquisition/collections/RBSC-INQ:COLLECTION/essays/RBSC-INQ:ESSAY_Autosdefe

Kurinsky, Samuel. "Jews and Navigation." *Hebrew History Federation.* http://www.hebrewhistory.info/factpapers/fp009_navigation.htm

PBS. *Heritage: Civilization and the Jews.* "Timeline." PBS.org http://www.pbs.org/wnet/heritage/timeline4.html

PBS. *When Worlds Collide: The Untold Story of the Americas after Columbus.* "Isabella and Ferdinand." Undated. http://www.pbs.org/kcet/when-worlds-collide/people/queen-isabella-and-king-ferdinand-i.html

Rubin, Nancy. *Isabella of Castile: The First Renaissance Queen.* Lincoln, NE: iUniverse, 2004.

Sacudeo, Jarob. "Types of Clothing of the Middle Ages." *Bright Hub Education,* December 27, 2011. http://www.brighthubeducation.com/history-homework-help/106277-types-of-clothing-worn-during-the-middle-ages/

Schloss, Rabbi Chaim. *2000 Years of Jewish History.* Jerusalem, Israel: Feldheim Publishers, 2002.

"Spain, the Jews, the Spanish Inquisition, and After." http://www.jackwhite.net/iberia/spain.html

"The Spanish Empire." *Spain Travel Guide.* http://www.spanish-fiestas.com/history/empire/

"Tisha B'AV." *The Jewish Community Center of Harrison.* August 2, 2012. http://www.jcch.org/index.php?option=com_content&view=article&id=580:tisha-bav&catid=36:Cantor&Itemid=81

On the Internet

"Spanish Inquisition" on Kids.net.au
    http://encyclopedia.kids.net.au/page/sp/Spanish_Inquisition

"The Middle Ages for Kids/The Inquisition"
    http://medievaleurope.mrdonn.org/inquisition.html

astrolabe—An astronomical instrument used for finding the height of the sun or stars above the horizon.

baptize—To dedicate a life to God and be purified.

caliph—A Muslim religious and political leader.

cathedral—A large Christian or Catholic church.

chamber pot—A bowl used as a toilet, especially at night.

cholent—A stew of beans, vegetables, and sometimes meat prepared before Shabbat but left to simmer and be enjoyed during the weekly day of rest.

confiscation—The taking of another's property or belongings, especially as a penalty.

conquistador—A Spanish conqueror.

Converso—A Jew who converted Christianity.

convert—To denounce one's religion and adopt a different one.

damask—A thick, heavy fabric usually with a pattern woven into it.

edict—A decree, or order by an authority.

familiar—One of the officers under the Inquisitor General's orders.

gargoyle—A carved animal face or figure on a building.

Hanukkah—A Jewish holiday that falls in November or December and celebrates the rededication of the Temple; the celebration lasts for eight days.

heretic—Anyone who goes against the established religion, attitude, or belief.

Islam—The religion of the Muslims.

lentil—A type of plant with small, edible seeds.

menorah—A Jewish lamp that holds seven or nine candles and is used to celebrate Hanukkah.

monarch—An absolute ruler.

Moor—A member of the group of Muslims that settled in Spain.

Passover—A Jewish holiday lasting a week or more that celebrates the Jews escape from Egypt in biblical times.

pestilence—A widespread, deadly disease.

privy—An outhouse or outdoor toilet.

quadrant—An instrument shaped like a quarter of a circle that sailors used for navigation.

rabbi—A Jewish scholar who rules on questions of Jewish law.

Seder—The traditional meal and story that celebrates the Jewish exodus from Egypt, usually held during Passover.

Shabbat—The Jewish day of rest, or Sabbath; it starts at sundown on Friday with the lighting of candles over dinner, and ends at sundown on Saturday.

Spanish mission—One of the Spanish forts built in newly conquered areas to spread the word of Christianity.

sultan—A king or ruler of a Muslim state.

Talmud—The body of Jewish law.

tapestry—A woven rug or carpet usually hung on inside walls of wealthier homes; the weaving often depicts a story or contains important symbols.

Torah—The five books of the Hebrew Bible.

tunic—A shirt that is usually sleeveless and is sometimes belted.